A Beautiful World

Also by James Norbury

Big Panda and Tiny Dragon

The Journey: A Big Panda and Tiny Dragon Adventure

The Cat Who Taught Zen

Following the Moon

A Beautiful World

James Norbury

MICHAEL JOSEPH

For my brother Alan.

The world is less beautiful without you.

Beauty is not the responsibility of the world
but of the viewer.

HOW TO USE THIS BOOK

You can use this book in three different ways:

A STORY

Simply read it start to finish, all at once or perhaps a few pages a day.

A THOUGHT FOR THE DAY

Open it at a random page and consider it over the course of your day. There are narrative sections in the book, so you might need to pick a new page if you get one of those.

A HELPER

Each chapter covers a different theme, so if you are facing a particular challenge at the moment there may be a chapter which could help. The chapters loosely cover the following ideas:

The Teahouse – No theme – page 7
The Ruins – Loss and living with the past – page 17
The Shore – Insignificance – page 31
The Mountains – Anger and finding peace – page 49
The Caverns – Fear and anxiety – page 65
The Swamp – Self-doubt – page 73
The Barrens – Nihilism and purposelessness – page 87
The Chasm – Separation and solitude – page 105
The Forest – Depression and feeling incomplete – page 125
A Beautiful World – Recognizing beauty where you are right now – page 141

The Teahouse

On the edge of the great ruins
stood an ancient teahouse.

One evening, two friends sheltered within its crumbling walls.

They drank hot tea and spoke of distant lands.

Big Panda took a sip and watched Tiny Dragon as he added more hot water to the pot.

'Have you ever looked inside that box you prepare the tea on?' he asked.

Tiny Dragon shook his head. 'Never,' he said. 'I don't even know if it opens.'

But now the idea was in his head, his curiosity immediately got the better of him. He moved the teapot and the tattered hessian cloth and began to cautiously examine the box.

It was a simple thing:
old and battered with rusted hinges
and a lock that had long been broken.

'I think I can open it,' squeaked Tiny Dragon,
clearly excited.

Gathering all his strength, he heaved at the lid.
The hinge groaned, cracked and suddenly gave way.

Tiny Dragon rammed his head into the box, peering into every corner, then emerged looking a little disappointed.

'Just an old piece of paper,' he harrumphed.

Big Panda took the paper and held it up to the candlelight.

'Hmmm…' he said.
'It's not just a piece of paper, it's a map.

And it claims to show the way to
The Most Beautiful Place in the World.'

Tiny Dragon sped across the room and shot up
Big Panda's back, peering around his head
to get a good look.

'We have to go,' he said. 'Can you even imagine
The Most Beautiful Place in the World?
Come on, let's pack.'

Big Panda smiled.

He knew it was late and that the clouds were gathering, but he also knew that once Tiny Dragon had set his mind on something, one way or another it was going to happen.

The Ruins

As the sun rose, Big Panda and Tiny Dragon found themselves among the ruins of a long-forgotten city.

As they wandered between the crumbling columns and shattered masonry, Tiny Dragon could not help but be drawn into the past, his mind dwelling on all he had lost, the frailty of life, and how all things would ultimately turn to dust.

'Nothing lasts for ever,' said Big Panda.

'Not even the pain you're feeling now.'

'Does my past control my future?' asked Tiny Dragon.

'It doesn't have to,' said Big Panda. 'It's you who steers the boat, not the wake it leaves behind.'

Bringing too much of the past with you can make it
very difficult to move forwards.

'Do you ever wonder what might have been?'
asked Tiny Dragon.

'No,' said Big Panda.
'There is a peace in knowing it could not
have happened any other way.'

So much ruin, so much loss,
yet still…so much beauty.

From the ancient ruins a tree took root.

Even in loss, life finds a way.

'Are you still struggling with the past?'
asked Big Panda.

'I visit it,' said Tiny Dragon.
'I learn from it, but I try not to be there too long.
Otherwise it would be very hard to be here, now,
with you, on this adventure.'

As night fell, they sat amid the serene desolation of the broken city, looking out at a sky that held a myriad of untold wonders.

Tiny Dragon took Big Panda's paw and smiled.

'I can't change the past, but we're here now and the world is waiting for us. I think I'm ready to move on.'

The Shore

The silence gave way to the distant sound
of waves lapping on the shore.

Tiny Dragon looked upon the vast, endless ocean
and felt so very small and insignificant.

How did he fit into this overwhelming world?

What difference did he really make to anything?

'I wish I could send the clouds away for you,'
said Tiny Dragon.

'You don't need to,' said Big Panda.
'You have helped me realize
how beautiful they are.'

'We would never have planned it like this,'
said Tiny Dragon,
staring out at the endless rain.

'No,' agreed Big Panda. 'But having you with me
makes it a moment
I would choose again and again.'

'Some of your cups are damaged,' said Big Panda.

'Yes,' said Tiny Dragon.
'But they are all perfect, even the broken ones.'

'I wish I was extraordinary,' said Tiny Dragon,
admiring a beautiful bird.

'You are,' said Big Panda. 'You are made of the same power
and wonder that flows through the mountains, the rivers,
the skies and even this bird. You don't need to become
something else – you are already a part of nature's wonder.'

'There will always be difficulties,' said Big Panda.
'But having a friend like you makes life a little bit easier.'

Those who care for others may never get
the thanks they deserve.
So, thank you.
Your love and kindness change the world
in ways you'll never see.

A tiny action in the right place can change everything.
Don't underestimate the effect
you can have on the world.

The world is so amazing, thought Tiny Dragon.
The huge mountains,
the wonderful trees, all the incredible
things people do and build.
It's easy to feel even tinier than I am.

Sometimes I have to remind myself…

I am enough.

'If I am enough,' said Tiny Dragon,
'why strive for anything?'

Big Panda took Tiny Dragon's hand in his huge paw.

'It is a wonderful thing to enjoy this world, to try new things, to push yourself, and succeed and fail. But none of these things will make you any more than you are right now.

Growth is not about becoming someone else, but unfolding who you've always been.'

'Do you ever think you should be doing more?'
asked Tiny Dragon.

Big Panda smiled.

'The flowers do not return more beautiful each spring.'

They didn't know quite where they were going;
they never really did.
But that didn't matter, because they found the
greatest fulfilment not in where they travelled,
but who they travelled with.

'The moon seems so small,' said Tiny Dragon,
'but it brightens the darkest night.
If I ever feel insignificant again,
I will think of the moon.'

The Mountains

The trail left the coast and rose steeply into the mountains.

As they climbed higher, icy rain and biting winds chilled Tiny Dragon to his core.

The universe just kept throwing one terrible thing after another at them.

The peace he had been feeling was replaced by frustration and anger.

'It's still so far to go,' said Tiny Dragon.
'I feel like we'll never get there.'

'Progress isn't always visible,' said Big Panda.
'Sometimes it feels like nothing is changing.
But the seeds you have planted are still growing,
ready to bloom when the time is right.'

High in the mountains, the monkey had been goading the tiger all day.

But every time the tiger tried to catch him, the monkey leapt into another tree.

'When someone angers you,' said Big Panda, 'consider this... It is not what they are doing *to* me, it's what they are doing *for* me. Without the monkey's help, how would you practise overcoming your anger? Isn't peace what you really want?'

'How are you so kind to everyone we meet?'
asked Tiny Dragon.

'I try to remember that each person is
facing a struggle I cannot see,' said Big Panda.
'Then it's not so difficult.'

Each time they stopped, Tiny Dragon would practise his little bamboo flute.

'I'll never get it,' huffed Tiny Dragon,
about to smash it on the ground.

'Peace doesn't come from avoiding things that
make you upset or angry,' said Big Panda,
'but from facing those things again and again,
and doing your best to choose peace each time.'

'But it's so overwhelming,' said Tiny Dragon frantically. 'There's so much to learn, so much to do, so much to…I just…'

'If you slow down and pay attention,' said Big Panda, 'you will find hidden within the most mundane tasks the peace that you are seeking.'

'I am sorry for getting angry,' said Tiny Dragon.

'There's no need to be sorry, Little One,' said Big Panda.
'Each time anger rises, it offers a chance to let go and,
if we do, we can start to find a deeper,
more lasting peace.'

'What if we never find The Most Beautiful Place
in the World?' asked Tiny Dragon, exasperated.

'In that case,' said Big Panda, 'we'll have had only the
journey itself, which is why we must do our best to savour
all of it – its twists and turns, the highs and lows,
however undesirable they might appear.'

'It's a long road to happiness,'
said Big Panda.

'Then why don't we start being happy right here?'
asked Tiny Dragon.

Tiny Dragon looked up at the sky, his mind awed
by the boundless wonder of the universe.

'Our differences seem so small,' he said.
'We should forgive more.'

Big Panda nodded.
'Peace is worth more than any grudge.'

The Caverns

The mountain trail eventually began to descend and, just as the map showed, a large cave opened out before them. But it was dark and cold, and eerie sounds echoed off its damp walls.

Fear and anxiety gripped Tiny Dragon as he stepped towards the unknown.

'I know you're scared,' said Big Panda.
'You cannot help that. But you have chosen not to let fear stop your journey and that shows great courage.'

'The world can be a dark place sometimes,'
said Tiny Dragon.

'But where it's darkest,' said Big Panda,
'your light will make the most difference.'

If you're in the dark,
someone else can lend you their light.

You can't keep it,
but you can use it to find your own light.

'I'm worried about tomorrow,' said Tiny Dragon.

'Tomorrow never comes,' said Big Panda.
'There is only today, and we've always dealt with today.'

Life is like a pot of tea.
Sometimes it's too much for one person.
Share it if you can.

'How is it you never seem worried?' asked Tiny Dragon.

'I have worried about many things in my life,'
said Big Panda, 'and few of them ever came to pass.
When you realize that, it makes it much easier to let
the world play out as it wants to.'

Tiny Dragon took a deep breath and felt the beginnings
of a new faith in the world as he stepped out into
the light of day.

The Swamp

The earth beneath their feet became waterlogged
and the trees bent crooked and leafless.

Tiny Dragon was consumed with self-doubt.
He knew he did not have the will to endure
this dying land.

'The doubts may never stop, Little One,
so it might be wise to learn to carry on anyway.'

'I keep starting things but giving up,' said Tiny Dragon.

Big Panda shook his head.

'You are here now, talking to me. So, no – you have not given up. You've just not quite found your stride.'

'Everyone else is going up the tree,' sighed Little Ant.

'Everyone else doesn't know what's best for you,'
said Big Panda.

'I think we're lost,' said Tiny Dragon.

'Follow your soul,' said Big Panda.
'Trust that it knows the way.'

'I'd like to write about our journey but don't know if I'm good enough,' sighed Tiny Dragon.

'The biggest mistake you'll make,' said Big Panda, 'is not even starting.'

'I feel I should be doing more,' said Tiny Dragon.

'Try to celebrate the things you have done,' said Big Panda, 'rather than regret the things you haven't.'

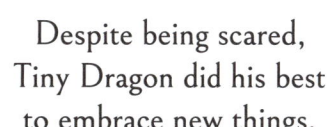

Despite being scared,
Tiny Dragon did his best
to embrace new things.

'I know you doubt yourself, Little One,
but there are people out there who can't believe
how amazing you are.'

The Barrens

'Sometimes I feel empty and without purpose,' said Tiny Dragon.

'Purposelessness isn't emptiness,' said Big Panda. 'Think of it as the freedom to wander, to explore and to let life unfold without any expectations.'

Tiny Dragon searched and searched
but couldn't find
what he was looking for.

'Perhaps it's already inside you?'
suggested Big Panda.

'I'm so tired,' said Tiny Dragon.
'I just don't know what to do.'

Big Panda smiled gently. 'Nature has a season for all things
– beginning, growth, reflection and rest.
We are part of nature, my little friend, and should
not be afraid to follow her good example.'

In a trail above the barren pass,
Tiny Dragon spotted something.
'Those ruins look incredible! Can we go there instead?'

'It's a few days' extra travel,' said Big Panda,
'but I don't see why not.'

Two days later they stood among the ruins.
'These old rocks aren't nearly as good close up.
But it looks amazing over there!' said Tiny Dragon,
pointing to the cliff they had just come from.

Big Panda sighed.

'Will it always be like this?' asked Tiny Dragon.

'No,' said Big Panda.
'The clouds will pass, the storm will end
and the trees will lose their leaves.
Change is one thing you can be certain of.'

'Do you like long journeys?' asked Tiny Dragon.

'The longer the better,' said Big Panda,
'as long as you're with me.'

'I don't know, Little One,' said Big Panda,
wrapping the little creature in his huge arms.
'I don't think such a thing is out there to be found.'

'So what do I do?' begged Tiny Dragon,
tears rolling down his face.

'You stop searching.
Close your eyes, watch your mind,
don't judge it – that's you – hidden but still there.
I think when you learn to see you,
the answers might start to come.'

A leaf never falls in the wrong place.

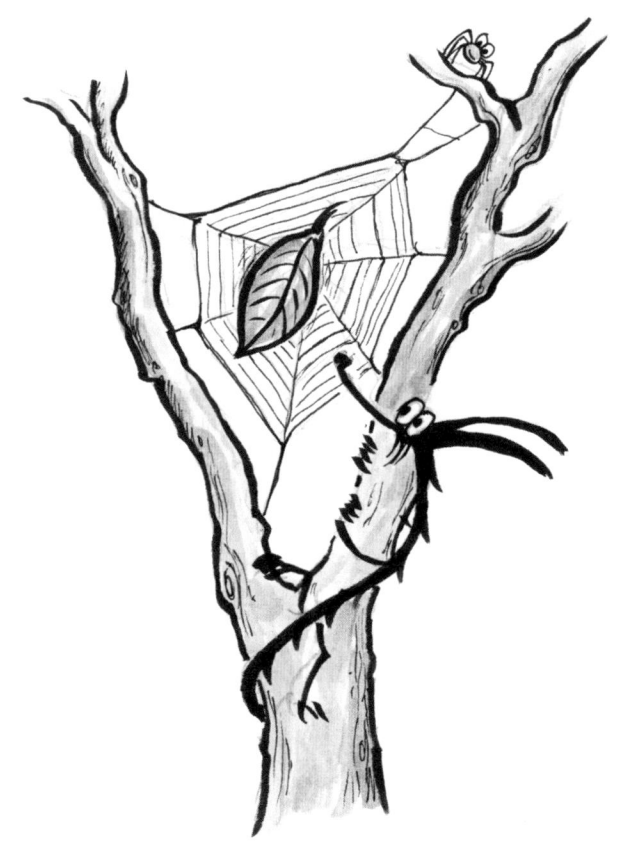

Trust that you are where you need to be.

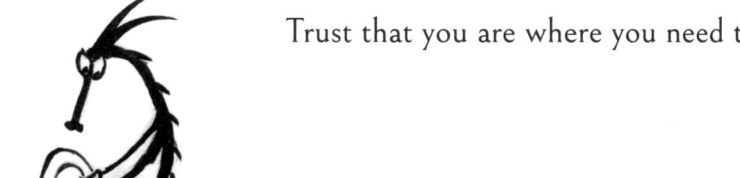

'I'm bored,' said Tiny Dragon.

Big Panda smiled.

'Maybe you are just a small step away from peace.'

'But I feel a sense of purpose would help.
A reason to get out of bed.
It would make me feel alive!'

'Then be still, feel the wind on your face,
listen to my words and breathe.
To be fully here – that is purpose.'

'If you want to make the very best tea in the world,
or find the most beautiful place, of course, you should try,'
said Big Panda.

'But if you try from a place of peace and presence you will
enjoy it all the more, and not be broken if you fail.'

'Is life passing us by while we sit here doing nothing?' asked Tiny Dragon.

'Life is sitting here,' said Big Panda.

The path led nowhere useful.

But not all paths are meant to.
Maybe in losing ourselves,
we might start to find ourselves.

The Chasm

One morning, they found that their path was blocked
by a great gorge that split the earth.

The bridge had seen better days and Big Panda
was concerned it wouldn't hold his bearishness.

Tiny Dragon climbed up on to the post
and looked across to the other side.
He took a few tentative steps on to the bridge.

And then there was a terrible tearing sound.
Before Tiny Dragon could leap back to safety the
old ropes gave way and the bridge split in two.

The section of bridge he was on swung away from the cliff.
He grabbed on tight and shut his eyes.

He could feel the wind rushing past him and splinters
of rotten wood clattering off his scaly body.

Tiny Dragon opened his eyes and saw he was on the opposite side of the chasm.

Far in the distance he could see Big Panda standing on the clifftop.

Summoning all his strength, he clambered up the broken bridge until he could haul himself to safety.

Each alone and with no idea where to go, Big Panda and Tiny Dragon had little choice but to carry on and trust that fate would guide them to the right path.

The flower still blooms,
even if you are too sad to see it.

Sometimes even the strongest people need a hand to hold.

Tiny Dragon was alone,
but he did not distract himself.
Instead, he sat with himself,
and slowy but surely,
began to find himself.

Big Panda had searched all day.

Now night had fallen and he worried about his little friend.

As he watched a shooting star arc across the heavens, he remembered… The universe would unfold as it was meant to. Faith took root in his heart and he knew they would be OK.

Different places…
Same moon…
Maybe we're not so far apart.

Solitude can be a painful place where we are forced to face ourselves.

But in that emptiness can be found a peaceful world,
where we can build and grow and begin to know ourselves.

Tired and lost, Big Panda was starting to give up hope
when something in the air caught his nose.

Smoke, with a note of fruit, and maybe something
earthy and fresh, with a hint of new grass.

Crashing through the undergrowth, he burst through
a copse of bamboo and there, in a clearing,
was Tiny Dragon making some tea.

'You made tea, what a clever idea.'

'Umm…yes…' said Tiny Dragon, sheepishly.

'Actually, I just needed a big hug,
and a cup of tea was the closest I could get.'

The best thing about your friend going away…

. . . is meeting them all over again.

'I'm so glad we're back travelling together,'
said Tiny Dragon.
'But sitting with myself, although difficult,
was still a journey I'm glad I took.

I discovered new worlds.
Worlds I could only have found on my own.'

The Forest

Together once more, Big Panda and Tiny Dragon were
soon struggling through a dark and tangled forest.
It wasn't long before they were lost.

For no reason he could fathom, Tiny Dragon felt
profoundly sad and a sense of incompleteness, as though
something important was missing from his life.

Something that would make all the difference.

Hopelessness whispers that you are
alone and unworthy. But it lies.

Even the darkest path will eventually
lead into the sunlight.

Deep in the forest, they stumbled across Green Dragon, who lived alone in a large cave. Tiny Dragon sighed. 'I wish I had a cave in the forest like Green Dragon.'

'Really?' asked Big Panda. 'When I was speaking to him, he said all he wanted was someone to share it with.'

'I wish I had a shell to hide in sometimes,'
said Tiny Dragon.

'It's very useful,' said the tortoise,
'but I've found that, now and then, you have to stick
your neck out to get where you want to go.'

'What an incredible tree,' said Tiny Dragon.

'Just like us,' said Big Panda, 'it grew imperfect, unusual and unique. That is why it is so beautiful.'

It's hard to even imagine there's light,
when we are so deep in darkness.

But it's there, so let's keep walking.

'Having you as a friend helps me so much with so many things,' said Tiny Dragon.

'And then I think of Green Dragon alone in his cave. I want to help him like you've helped me.'

'You came back a long way to see me,' said Green Dragon.

'Every new friend offers a whole new beginning,' grinned Tiny Dragon. 'Like a new world ready to be discovered.'

What seems hopeless one day
can look slightly different the next.

The darkness of the forest began to shift as
sunlight trickled through the canopy above and
the melody of birdsong filled the air.

Tiny Dragon's heart lifted.
He ran a hand through Big Panda's fur.

'I know that even after the darkest night,
the sun always rises,' said Tiny Dragon,
'but no one reminds me of that more than you.'

When they finally broke out of the trees,
they beheld a view so magnificent
they were both lost for words.

A
Beautiful
World

'This place is unbelievable,'
gasped Tiny Dragon.

'This tree,' he said. 'Look at it. So tall, and the way the branches twist and turn. It's just magical.'

But as he ran his hand over the textured bark, he noticed it felt the same as the bark on the tree that grew by the stream near their home.

This tree was much taller, and the branches remarkably twisted, but it seemed to be the same type of tree.

Big Panda was captivated by a verdant, thick moss that was growing over an ancient statue of a fox.

Up close it was like an incredible miniature forest.

But the longer he looked, the more he saw the moss was the same variety as the one that covered the stone steps of their temple.

It was much less noticeable, but no less exquisite.

A great roar made them both look up. High above them,
perched on a rocky cliff, was a great beast,
its colourful fur shimmering in the morning sunlight.

Tiny Dragon was awed by the creature,
but as it moved off into the trees,
its movements reminded him of the little
grey cat who visited their home each morning.

The cat was smaller, perhaps,
with very different colours,
but no less beautiful.

'I don't understand,' said Tiny Dragon.

'It's kind of the same as back home – amazing but no more amazing – so why do I feel so alive, so…present?'

'Back at the temple, the cat, the tree, the moss – they are all miracles, each deserving of our full attention, but we have forgotten how to look,' said Big Panda.

Wherever you call your home is alive with wonder.
You've just forgotten.

Tiny Dragon sat in silence,
taking in all the tiny details around him.
A tear rolled down his cheek.

'It was beautiful all along, wasn't it?'

'Yes,' said Big Panda kindly.

Tiny Dragon sighed. 'So why couldn't I see it?'

'What you have experienced has shown you what is
possible – it has made you aware of what was there
all along.

We have had a difficult journey, but perhaps our hardships
have not been without lessons and gifts.

Amid ruins and loss, we learnt acceptance.

Confronted by a vast shore, we found our worth.

Within the mountains, our anger led to peace.

In dark caves, through our fears we developed courage.

As we journeyed through the swamp,
our doubt gave way to trust.

Lost in the barrens, we found purpose
through embracing the present.

We were parted by a chasm and felt the pain
of loneliness, but we learnt the value of our own
company as well as the pleasure of companionship.

And as we ventured into the darkness of the forest,
we found faith in the light within and beyond us.

With each step, our ability to see beauty
and feel compassion has grown.'

When the tree waves its leaves,
it's calling for your attention.

When a bird sings,
it's reminding you to stop and listen.

As the cold mountain wind scours your cheek,
it is reminding you to feel.

Nature is your friend,
and all the time it is calling you back to yourself.

Be patient, look for the signs and give the world
the attention it deserves.

Tiny Dragon reached down and ran his finger across a dark, shiny leaf.

And in that moment, the world around him seemed fiercely alive.

He wrapped his arms around Big Panda, his face smothered in thick, damp fur. The great bear smelled of wind and rain and dark, primal forests, and his eyes shone jet in the dwindling light.

Tiny Dragon had never felt so safe…so loved.

Tiny Dragon released his friend and stepped back,
taking in the soaring mountains, majestic waterfalls
and towering trees.

They were awe-inspiring, but no more of a miracle than the
small ebony scales that ran over the backs of his tiny hands.

As the sun dipped behind the mountains and a cool
wind stirred, Big Panda, tired but content,
bedded down into the long grass.

'You know…' said Tiny Dragon, snuggling into his fur…

'We've travelled to so many amazing places I've lost count, but I like it here best of all.'

AFTERWORD

I often get asked how I ended up creating these books, so I will briefly explain it here.

I worked as an artist and writer for about twenty years. I was extremely unsuccessful and spent most of my life earning very small amounts of money. But I was very determined; it was the only path for me, so I persisted.

Eventually, though, I'd had enough and I was worn out by the whole process. I decided to pack it in and become an odd-jobs man. (There are a lot of skills you learn when you have no money.)

But before that, I decided to do one last project, which I had been planning for years but had never gotten around to.

Because I had struggled a lot with mental health, I'd spent many years studying spirituality, especially Buddhism, and it had helped me enormously. I wanted to take the concepts I had learnt and share them with others in a very accessible way, as I know many people don't have the inclination to read large, dry books in order to get a few useful ideas.

I decided single-panel, concise images were the best format, and I would share them on social media. Interestingly, it was a project I started with absolutely no interest in making any money from. It seems the universe approved of this approach.

The picture above (and reimagined on page 90) is the very first Big Panda and Tiny Dragon picture I ever drew. Tiny Dragon was different back then and I couldn't draw pandas at all — I still struggle with them sometimes.

But I thought, I'll give it a go. I painted these pictures on photocopier paper with ink and a cheap brush. I did it pretty fast as I thought no one would ever see them and I didn't want to waste too much time.

This picture still has massive significance as every book I write is simply my own way of confronting myself and digging below the surface to find out what's really going on. Initially, I thought my obstacles would be unique and the things I wrote about wouldn't apply to others, but over time I have learnt that most of us deal with the very same issues, albeit dressed up in slightly different clothes.

This book that you are holding is my fifth book and I can gratefully confirm that what I set out to do really does work, both for me and for the many readers who write to tell me how much the books have changed their lives.

But the books are just signposts; they point in the right direction. Sometimes they wake you up and remind you of things you had forgotten, or they allow you to look at an issue with fresh eyes, but the work always comes down to the individual.

No book or nugget of wisdom will set you free. I believe, as I have tried to explain in my work, that liberation comes from insight – getting to know yourself and your thoughts.

There are thousands of people trying to tell you how to be happy. Perhaps some of their suggestions work. I have not personally encountered a book or a video that bestows happiness upon the viewer.

But the purpose of this book is not to make you happy; it's simply to give you a little poke and help you remember that the world can be beautiful if you choose to look at it that way. I live in a city that was bombed and hastily rebuilt – not the most obviously scenic place – yet all around me there are wonderful sights: hypnotic textures and colours in the concrete, delicate curls of peeling paint, rain pooling in the gutters, tiny plants struggling through the tarmac. I have learnt to see wonder in the mundane and it can make every day beautiful. I hope this book might help you do the same.

Very first concept drawings of the two characters.

AUTHOR'S NOTE

I debated whether to include this, but I will as it is very important to the nature of the book.

Approximately halfway through the creation of this book my brother Alan died. It was very sudden. He was only fifty-nine, and I know everyone says this, but he was one of the sweetest souls I have ever known. He was born deaf and had severe learning difficulties. If you can imagine a kind eleven-year-old boy in the body of a grown-up, that was him. At his funeral the undertaker said he'd never seen so many people at the crematorium in his career – a testament to Alan's nature.

Alan loved to draw and was one of the purest artists I have ever met. He had no interest in money, and the fact that my father and I are both professional artists did not intimidate him in the slightest. He would proudly show us his work and usually then gift it to people.

You can probably imagine that midway through writing a book called *A Beautiful World*, this event might have caused me to question what I was doing. And yes, for a short while it did. But I have chosen not to see ugliness; I have decided to see beauty – in Alan, his pictures and in the memories I have of him. And it is almost as though I can see even more beauty in the world when forced to confront the ephemeral nature of life.

Ring-tailed lemur by Alan.

ACKNOWLEDGEMENTS

I would like to thank the following people for their help and support over the past year.

Ruth, as ever. I know how much you do so I can focus on my work. Thank you.

Dan and Emma, this was an awkward book to write and your skills and thoroughness really helped make it into something special. Thank you.

Adriana, you are such a positive cheerleader for me. Thank you.

Ludo, thank you for your enthusiasm and for doing all the administrative work that keeps things going. I really appreciate it.

Andy Rosser-Davies and Paul Davies for their undying love of their arts (guitar and karate respectively). Seeing the passion you guys have and your desire to share it is endlessly inspiring.

Thank you also to the team at Penguin Michael Joseph for all your work making the books look beautiful and getting them out to customers: Alice Gordge, Sarah Fraser, Lee Motley and Lily Evans. And Eva, thank you for sending me all the books and bits and pieces from Penguin and for the beautifully written note in each one. Thanks also to everyone in the PRH rights team who have worked so hard to get my books out to the world.

I would also like to thank all my international publishers for their continued support of my work.

Penguin Michael Joseph

UK | USA | Canada | Ireland | Australia
India | New Zealand | South Africa

Penguin Michael Joseph is part of the Penguin Random House group of companies whose addresses can be found at global.penguin-randomhouse.com

Penguin Random House UK,
One Embassy Gardens, 8 Viaduct Gardens,
London SW11 7BW

penguin.co.uk

First published in Great Britain by
Michael Joseph, 2025
001

Text copyright © James Norbury, 2025
Illustration copyright © James Norbury, 2025

The moral right of the author has been asserted

Penguin Random House values and supports copyright. Copyright fuels creativity, encourages diverse voices, promotes freedom of expression and supports a vibrant culture. Thank you for purchasing an authorized edition of this book and for respecting intellectual property laws by not reproducing, scanning or distributing any part of it by any means without permission. You are supporting authors and enabling Penguin Random House to continue to publish books for everyone. No part of this book may be used or reproduced in any manner for the purpose of training artificial intelligence technologies or systems. In accordance with Article 4(3) of the DSM Directive 2019/790, Penguin Random House expressly reserves this work from the text and data mining exception.

Set in Bauer Bellefair
Colour reproduction by Altaimage Ltd
Printed and bound in Germany by Mohn Media GmbH

The authorized representative in the EEA is
Penguin Random House Ireland,
Morrison Chambers, 32 Nassau Street, Dublin
D02 YH68

A CIP catalogue record for this book is available from the British Library

ISBN: 978-0-241-75752-9

Penguin Random House is committed to a sustainable future for our business, our readers and our planet. This book is made from Forest Stewardship Council® certified paper.